BOATS AND SHIPS

TRAVELING MACHINES

Jason Cooper

Rourke Enterprises, Inc.
Vero Beach, Florida 32964

PHOTO CREDITS

© Lynn M. Stone: all photos except p. 18 © James P. Rowan

LIBRARY OF CONGRESS
Library of Congress Cataloging-in-Publication Data
Cooper, Jason, 1942-
   Boats and ships / by Jason Cooper.
   p.   cm. — (Traveling machines)
   Includes index.
   Summary: Examines the history, varieties, and uses of boats
and ships.
   ISBN 0-86592-492-9
   1. Boats and boating—Juvenile literature.   2. Ships—Juvenile
literature. [1. Boats and boating. 2. Ships.] I. Title.
II. Series: Cooper, Jason, 1942-   Traveling machines.
VM150.C63   1991
623.8'2—dc20   90-26924
                             CIP
                             AC

TABLE OF CONTENTS

SHIPS AND BOATS

Ships and boats, sometimes called vessels, sail on bodies of water. Ships are larger than boats and often used at sea.

Most boats are used for pleasure. Some ships are used for pleasure, but most are used for freight transport, warfare, and other jobs.

Boats and ships are built on a hollow body shell called a **hull.** The **rudder,** a flat section of steel or other material under the hull, helps steer the vessel.

Fishing trawler and pleasure boats in Monterey, California

EARLY SHIPS AND BOATS

The first boats did not have hulls or rudders. They were probably made of logs tied together. Hollowed logs, called dugouts, and canoes made of tree bark were also among early boats.

Boats with sails were developed at least 5,000 years ago by the Egyptians. For centuries, people all over the world used wooden sailboats.

A steam-powered boat appeared in 1807. The first iron sailing ship was the *Vulcan*, made in England in 1818.

Whaleship Charles W. Morgan, *built in 1841, now at Mystic Seaport, Connecticut*

MODERN SHIPS

Ships made of steel and powered by engines rapidly replaced iron sailing ships in the late 1800s and early 1900s. These new ships were stronger, safer, and cheaper to operate.

In 1954, the U.S. Navy's **submarine** *Nautilus* became the world's first atomic-powered ship. Most ships today burn oil, but several warships in major navies are powered by atomic energy.

Ships are becoming larger and more **automated.** Computers now help captains operate their vessels.

9

U.S.S. Nautilus, *retired at Groton, Connecticut*

BOATS FOR FUN

Many kinds of boats—**kayaks,** canoes, rowboats, sailboats, houseboats, **catamarans,** and motorboats—are used for pleasure.

Canoes, rowboats, and kayaks are powered by people using paddles or oars. Sailboats are powered by wind. Motorboats usually have outboard engines mounted on the back or **stern** of the boat.

Boats are usually made of wood, fiberglass, aluminum, or steel.

Most boats are less than 20 feet long. Larger pleasure boats include **yachts** and cabin cruisers.

Outboard-powered motorboat, Bahama Islands

Freighter docked at Port of Miami

Car ferry in Miami, Florida

SAILBOATS

Today's sailboats are different from the first Egyptian sailboats. Little by little, changes were made in hull designs and rigging. The rigging includes the sails, the poles **(masts)** that hold the sails, and the ropes that help control the sails.

Sailing vessels grew faster, larger, and more steady in the water. Around 1300 A.D., rudders were added. During the 1800s, fast sailing ships with up to 35 sails were built.

Sailboats were once used for long-distance travel, warfare, and whaling, but now most sailboats are used for pleasure.

Sailboats on Connecticut River, Essex, Connecticut

WORKING SHIPS AND BOATS

Many types of ships are designed for hauling goods and other special jobs. Some of them are longer than two football fields!

Freighters carry lumber, coal, automobiles, and other goods. Huge tankers carry oil or other liquids.

Ferries transport autos and people from one **port,** or landing, to another. Large ferries may carry 350 cars and 800 passengers.

Tugs help ships into harbors and tow flat boats, called barges. Lobster boats and fishing **trawlers** are large boats used to catch seafood.

Tug with cruise ship, Miami, Florida

WARSHIPS

Naval ships, or warships, are used in warfare. Their crews of sailors can fire weapons at airplanes, other ships, and targets on land.

The first warships were long wooden boats called **galleys.** The Egyptians first used galleys nearly 5,000 years ago.

In the 1300s, the first warships with guns on their decks were built.

Modern naval ships include aircraft carriers, cruisers, destroyers, frigates, battleships, and submarines for undersea.

Various warships are armed with guns, missiles, torpedoes, and warplanes.

Battleship U.S.S. Alabama

PASSENGER SHIPS

Most of today's large passenger vessels are cruise ships. They are floating hotels and restaurants.

Cruise ships usually take passengers to several ports on a voyage that lasts from three to seven days. Several cruise ships travel between Florida and islands in the Caribbean Sea.

Ocean liners are giant passenger ships that travel across the sea. Today people usually travel overseas by airplane rather than by ship. Famous liners like the *Queen Mary* and *United States* have been retired from service because they couldn't attract enough passengers.

Cruise ship Nordic Empress, *Miami, Florida*

THE WONDER OF SHIPS

When ancient people went down to the shores of their land, they did not know what lay beyond the sea. Ships showed explorers the wonder of new lands.

Today the magic of boating is found not only in travel to new lands. Powerboat owners know the wonder of dazzling speed on water. Weekend sailboaters know the wonder of wind-filled sails and the *swish* of a sharp **bow** cutting quiet seas.

For anyone who boards a vessel, wonder still awaits.

Glossary

automated (AW tow may ted) — run by a machine

bow (BOW) — the front end of a boat or ship

catamaran (KAT ah mar an) — a type of boat with side-by-side twin hulls

galley (GAL ee) — a long, low, wooden ship powered by oars and sails

hull (HULL) — the main body of a ship

kayak (KI ak) — a light, portable boat with a frame covered by skin or fabric

mast (MAST) — a long pole rising from a ship deck; used to support rigging

port (PORT) — a harbor town visited by ships

rudder (RUH der) — a flat structure attached under a ship's hull to help steer

stern (STERN) — the rear end of a boat

submarine (SUB mar een) — a vessel designed for undersea use

trawler (TRAW ler) — a fishing boat that drags a large net called a trawl

yacht (YAHT) — a large, graceful, sharp-bowed boat used for pleasure cruising and racing

INDEX